Around Highworth and Faringdon

IN OLD PHOTOGRAPHS

Eighteenth-century print, showing a view of Faringdon from the west.

Around Highworth and Faringdon

IN OLD PHOTOGRAPHS

GRAHAM TANNER

Alan Sutton Publishing Limited
Phoenix Mill · Far Thrupp · Stroud
Gloucestershire

First Published 1994

Copyright © Graham Tanner

British Library Cataloguing in Publication Data.
A catalogue record for this book is available from
the British Library.

ISBN 0–7509–0855–6

Typeset in 9/10 Sabon.
Typesetting and origination by
Alan Sutton Publishing Limited.
Printed in Great Britain by
Ebenezer Baylis, Worcester.

Contents

Introduction

The title of this collection of old photographs may come as something of a surprise to the people of both Highworth and Faringdon. Although separated by only some 6 miles, the two ancient market towns appear at first sight to have little in common. The River Cole, which separates not only Wiltshire and Berkshire but also the Highworth and Faringdon Rural District Councils, has over the years acted effectively as both a physical and a cultural boundary. However, the histories of these two medieval towns, the influence of which was considerable in the Middle Ages, certainly run parallel to one another. The markets of the towns were each of great importance: that of Highworth was at one time the largest in Wiltshire, while the Faringdon market was of considerable note, particularly for barley, in western Berkshire and eastern Wiltshire.

The Civil War was visited upon both towns. In the case of Highworth the fortified church of St Michael was surrendered to parliamentary forces under Fairfax on 27 June 1645 by Major Hen of the Royal Garrison. For Faringdon, however, the Civil War became more a war of attrition. Faringdon House was a royal garrison, of which Sir Marmaduke Rawdon was appointed governor. In 1645 the governor of the garrison was a Roger Burgess, who had the distinction of repulsing the conqueror of Marston Moor and Naseby. Cromwell attacked Faringdon House with some six hundred men, and in the following year an equally unsuccessful attack was made under the command of Sir Robert Pye, who held a commission in the parliamentarian army. Sir Robert had the dubious pleasure of attacking the house and manor of which he was the proprietor. Such is the fortune of war, but happily not everyone is obliged to attempt to destroy his own home. The town suffered enormous damage, many houses were destroyed by fire, and the church steeple was beaten down by the parliamentary artillery. Faringdon was one of the last places that held out for the royalists, and not until the king's cause was hopeless did the garrison surrender, in June 1646.

Together, the Civil War and the plague were largely responsible for the decline of Highworth's market, with trade being transferred to Swindon. However, that of Faringdon survived the calamities of the Civil War and throughout the eighteenth century remained a market of some note. The coming of the railways in the nineteenth century further operated to the disadvantage of both towns. Neither was to feature on a main line, and the branch lines were relatively late in arriving in both cases. The influence of the Faringdon market began to decline, and by the late nineteenth century it was reduced to a trifling trade, with Newbury becoming the recipient of Faringdon's earlier trade. The effect of the railway on Highworth was even more traumatic – with the advent of the Great Western Railway Works at Swindon, the relative decline of Highworth became assured. The market virtually ceased to exist, and the first signs of Highworth as a dormitory for Swindon began to emerge.

The changes of the twentieth century, in particular the improved provision of public transport (albeit a journey by public transport from Highworth to Faringdon, or vice versa, is still somewhat problematic) and the ever-increasing popularity of the motor car, have done nothing to reverse the decline of the two towns. Amazingly, in 1839 there was a stagecoach between Highworth and Faringdon with six coaches per week, and in 1675 this was part of the 'pack horse' route from Oxford to Bristol surveyed by John Ogilby. By this time both towns had taken on their role of being pleasant dormitories for Swindon, and in the case of Faringdon for Oxford also. Sadly, along with this new role there was an accelerating decline in the commercial and industrial activities of the towns. The photographs assembled here clearly show thriving shopping facilities together with a wide range of country crafts and industries, many of which are now just memories among the older inhabitants. I hope that a celebration of the area's past may do a little to halt, or at the worst to slow down, the apparent desire of the 'city fathers' to turn this beautiful and bountiful area of the Vale of White Horse into one of William Cobbett's

A postcard dating from the early part of the century. The views shown include St Michael's parish church (centre) and Cricklade Road (top left).

The Town Hall and Crown Hotel, Market Place, Faringdon, in the 1980s.

despised urban 'wems'. In Cobbett's *Rural Rides* of 1826, in which he visited both Highworth and Coleshill, he comments most favourably on both the countryside and the people there, being 'detained at Highworth . . . by company that I liked very much'.

To those who love the towns and villages of this part of the Vale of White Horse, may I please make an appeal. Time is running out for the recording of the social history of the late nineteenth and early twentieth centuries. If you have memories, photographs or ephemera from this period that have not been recorded, please consider contacting your local historical society or me. In particular, material on entertainment – fairs, fêtes, etc. – and the war years, especially the evacuation to this area in 1939, is very thin. Your help would be much appreciated. Thank you.

SECTION ONE

Highworth

Aerial view of St Michael's parish church, High Street and Vicarage Lane, Highworth, *c.* 1930.

St Michael's parish church, *c*. 1950, decorated for the celebration of Harvest Festival, looking towards the west door.

Silver-gilt pre-Reformation chalice of 1534, corresponding to that at Trinity College, Oxford, showing our Lord as the 'Man of Sorrows'.

St Michael's parish church choir, early 1950s. Third row (seated), left to right: E. Gerring, -?-, E. German, Mr Mant, Sir T. Noel Arkell (churchwarden), Revd F.R. Webb MA (vicar), Revd Langmaid (curate), Mr G. Harris (organist), -?-, -?-, M. Mant.

Norman tympanum above the south door of St Michael's parish church, believed by Arthur Mee, author of *The King's England–Wiltshire*, to represent David fighting the lion.

High Street, probably late 1920s. Willis's grocers is on the far right.

High Street, early twentieth century.

High Street, late 1920s or early 1930s.

Christmas illuminations in High Street, *c.* 1970.

Market Place and High Street from the east, early 1950s. The Saracen's Head (left) still has its illuminated sign, which was introduced by Arkell's Brewery in the late 1930s.

Percy Chick (Builders) Ltd's fleet of vehicles outside the firm's offices, Sheep Street, *c.* 1960. This building was originally the Swan Inn, which had closed by 1871. On 16 October 1740 the Swan Inn was the venue for a wrestling match between Berkshire and Gloucestershire, when 'for the Encouragement of the Gamesters, the Landlord . . . will give Two Guineas to that side which shall throw Three Falls out of the Five, and a Half-a-Crown to every Man that throws a Fall'.

Market Place, *c.* 1910. The Rifleman's public house is on the far left, while Thomas the builders and Boulton's grocers are in the centre.

Market Place, mid-1950s.

Sheep Street from Cherry Orchard, before the First World War.

Swindon Street from the Centre, *c.* 1920.

Swindon Street, 1920s. Little has changed, with the exception of what is now Highworth Fish Shop, where the dormer windows have been removed and the roof lifted.

Swindon Street, late 1930s. This photograph was taken at approximately 5.10 p.m. on a sunny March day. The bus queue for the 5.15 p.m. bus to Swindon is forming by the lime trees outside Ashman's butchers shop. The outside gate to the Co-Op, leaning against the wall to the left of the shop, is ready to be locked in place.

Cricklade Road from the Centre, *c.* 1946. By this time the advertisement hoardings at the road's junction with Swindon Street had been removed.

Cricklade Road from the west, 1930s.

The Centre, 1920s.

Humphry's cycle shop (right) and private school (left), Swindon Street, c. 1912. The shop is now Sammy's fish and chip shop. On the reverse of this postcard the date of the school restarting after the Christmas holiday is given as 'Monday next Jan 18th'.

Congregational Church, High Street, before 1940. The iron railings were removed in 1940, ostensibly to assist the war effort.

Primitive Methodist Church, The Elms, *c.* 1920. This is now the Silver Threads Hall. The church was erected in 1850. For many years it was the head of a circuit, and was referred to in the *Swindon Centenary Souvenir Handbook* as 'a city set on a hill'.

The Rose & Crown public house, 1872. Later this building underwent extensive modernization. The adjoining cottages (left) in the Green were demolished in around 1936 and were replaced by the present somewhat unprepossessing houses.

Bowly's steam lorry. Bowly's were Swindon brewers, and used this lorry for deliveries of beer to The Rose & Crown during the 1920s and early 1930s.

The Rampant Cat public house, Redland, *c*. 1950. This was the property of Arkell's Brewery. The licence was transferred to the County Ground Hotel, Swindon, in 1897, as a result of James Arkell of Redlands Court objecting to the noisy conduct of the premises.

The Freke Arms, Swanborough, *c*. 1930. Despite appearing to be the only reason for the existence of Hannington station, The Freke dates back to 1839 and carries the arms of the Hussey-Freke family of Hannington Hall.

Cherry Orchard, looking south from the approximate site of the Highworth Gas Company's works, *c.* 1930. The council houses (left) were built in the 1920s.

Eastrop Hill from the Coleshill road, *c.* 1930, before the building of Kilminster's shop. Hungerford Barn is on the right.

Cherry Orchard, 1901. Woolford's wheelwrights yard is at the thatched house on the far right.

Paradise Row, Westrop, *c.* 1930.

Looking down Brewery Street, *c.* 1970, before realignment of the roads.

Brewery Street, *c.* 1970, before realignment.

The Fox Inn and Brewery Street, *c.* 1960, before the realignment of Brewery Street and the construction of the Fox roundabout. The old blacksmith's forge appears left of centre.

Swindon Street and The Fox, *c.* 1970, before the road was changed.

The Green, Swindon Street and The Fox, *c.* 1970, before the construction of the roundabout.

The Green, *c.* 1970, including Wheeler's marine stores, before demolition.

Reddown Bungalow. This was one of the few smallholdings set up around Highworth for returning servicemen after the First World War. Fennells Farm on the Shrivenham road was another.

Westrop Farm. This building dates from the seventeenth century, with evidence of even earlier habitation in the area.

Watercolour of Wrag Barn from the Shrivenham road. This picture is by Bill Bartrop and is from the author's collection.

The Queen's, High Street, on the occasion of army manoeuvres, 1909.

Highworth Fair at the Recreation Ground, The Elms, *c.* 1950.

Watercolour of the Lammas Fair, 1946. This picture is by Eric Chick and shows a view of the fair from the family home in Sheep Street. This was probably the last year of total steam fairs, before war surplus diesel generators replaced the showman's engines.

Highworth Guides outside the home of Mr and Mrs Mant, Westrop, *c.* 1950. Those present include ? Mant (standing, left) and Beryl Woodbridge (also standing).

Highworth Guide company with Rangers parading in Market Place, *c.* 1950.

Highworth Scouts, Weymouth, 1937. This trip to Weymouth took place during the Scouts' camp at West Bay, Dorset. Left to right: F. Higgs, Ian Trewhella (ASM), R. Fitchett, -?-, Mrs H.M. Tanner, W. Gorton, W. Tidmarsh (with head turned), Vivian Trewhella (ASM), J. Slack.

Guard of Honour of Highworth Scouts at the wedding of Muriel Tanner and Richard White, at St Michael's parish church, 1943.

Royal Antediluvian Order of Buffaloes (RAOB) Commemoration Service, Market Square, *c.* 1927.

Ernest Woodbridge, the saddler of High Street, wearing the regalia of the RAOB, *c.* 1920.

Concert party, Council School, c. 1912. This is believed to be the first 'flash' photograph taken in Highworth.

Eric and Bill Woodbridge with their dance band, c. 1937. Local dance bands were in considerable demand for the regular programme of dances held during the pre-war period in the Council School. The school is now Southfields Junior School.

Highworth Town Band, 1911. The venue is unknown.

Highworth Silver Band, leading the carnival procession in High Street, late 1940s.

Staff of Hill's wheelwrights, Brewery Street, *c.* 1935. Back row, left to right: E. Davis, G. Hill, M. Farmilo, E. King, H. Smith, T. Woodward. Middle row: F. Barrett, A. Hill, T. Hill. Front row: W. Hill, C. Alsopp.

'Darkie' Breakspeare with donkeys and grandchildren in Brewery Street, before its realignment.

The Routledge and Boulton families in a coach-and-four for a family outing, 1890s.

Coronation celebrations for King Edward VII and Queen Alexandra, Market Place, 1911.

The photographs on pages 40 to 43 mostly show caricatures of the candidates for the 1913 Parish Council Election. All but one of them cannot be identified.

Ernest Booth (right), headmaster of the Council School, is the only candidate who can be positively identified. He was universally referred to as 'General Booth', because he had the same name as the founder of the Salvation Army.

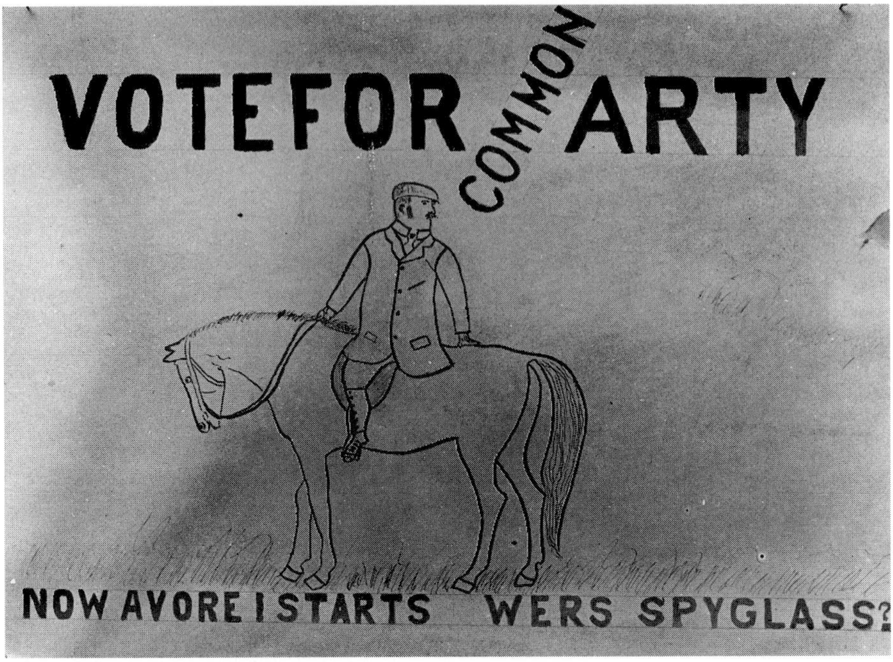

The reference to 'Spyglass' is explained in the caption below.

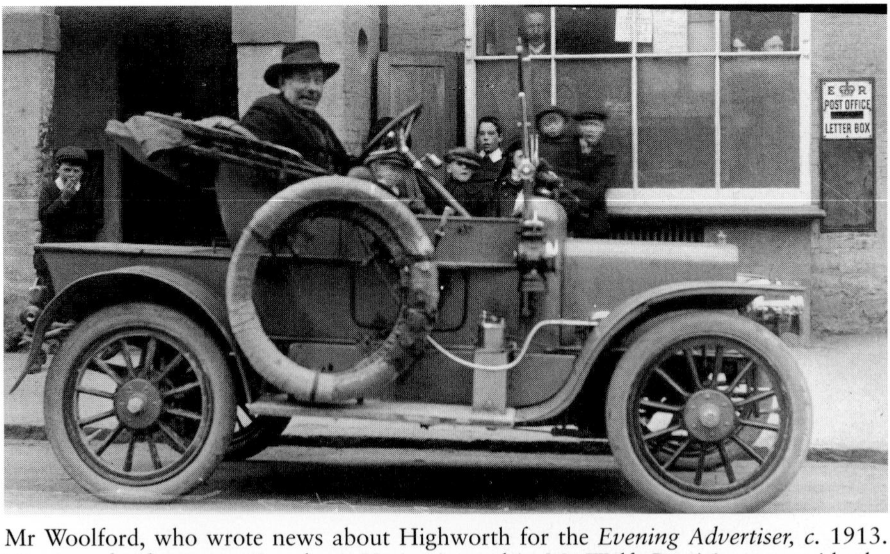

Mr Woolford, who wrote news about Highworth for the *Evening Advertiser, c.* 1913. His *nom de plume* was 'Spyglass'. He is pictured in Mr Wolfe-Barrie's car outside the post office, High Street.

Pupils and staff of Highworth National School, *c.* 1920.

Pupils and staff of Highworth Council School, 1919.

MEMBER'S TICKET.

HIGHWORTH
Literary and Scientific Institution.

Admit_____to the

Evening Lectures, 1857.

No. _____   **EDGAR E. SALMON,**
HON. SEC.

Not Tranferrable.

Membership ticket for the Highworth Literary and Scientific Institution, 1857. Lectures were given on a number of educational and cultural topics.

From the
HIGHWORTH KNITTING PARTY

Greetings to

L.A.C. Percy Willis. R.A.F.

with thanks and gratitude

for your Service in the World War

Token of thanks given by the Highworth Knitting Party to returning ex-servicemen after the Second World War.

Highworth Council School Netball Team, *c.* 1932. The girls are wearing the traditional black-and-white striped shirts.

Highworth Council School Football Team, *c.* 1932.

Highworth Town Football Club, *c.* 1960. Back row, left to right: ? Harris, E. Smith, P. Webb, R. Haines, P. Guy, B. Smith. Front row: R. Smith, J. Smith, ? Lewis, -?-, P. Brown.

Highworth Town Football Club, 1971. That year they were winners of the Dr Elliot Cup for the third time. Back row, left to right: J. New, S. Crowley, D. Smith, J. Pymer, R. Haines, K. Smith, P. Webb, B. Hobbs, A. Haines. Front row: M. Scholes, M. Gardner, P. Hillier, R. Cooper, P. Brown.

Highworth Town Football Club, 1907/8.

Although in no way specific to Highworth, this comic postcard of sport in Highworth is very appropriate. In the 1920s, Highworth Town Football Club were in trouble with the Football Association over behaviour at matches.

Highworth Town Football Club, 1957. Team members are celebrating winning the Wiltshire Junior Cup that year. Those present include P. Guy, C. Rayson, J. Smith (drinking from the cup), E. Smith and F. Ockwell (standing, rear).

Westrop Wanderers Football Team, c. 1945. Back row, left to right: -?-, K. Whittaker, P. Webb. Front row: -?-, T. Dean, B. Smith.

John Mapson (back row, centre) of Swindon Street played in goal for Sunderland against Preston North End in the FA Cup Final of 1937, winning 3–1. John had previously played for Holy Rood School, Swindon Boys, Highworth Town and Swindon Town.

Gorse Hill Trinity Football Club in the paddock opposite Westhill House, 1922. The team are pictured before a Borough League match against Westrop Rovers.

Highworth Wolves Cycle Speedway, Glebe Field, 1949. This is the start of a heat. Brian Smith is on the far right.

Highworth Wolves Cycle Speedway. Brian Smith is placed second at this stage.

Highworth Wolves Cycle Speedway, *c.* 1950. Back row, left to right: R. Coombs, H. Gorton, K. Whittaker, P. Webb, M. Haddock. Front row: -?-, B. Smith, T. Dean.

The opening of the Highworth swimming pool, April 1968. The pool was the culmination of the wartime 'Welfare Home Fund' and was in part the brainchild of Jack Silk, whose photograph is superimposed.

Highworth Bowls Club, *c.* 1960. Those present include E. Drew, P. Silk, F. Turner, W. Cook, E. Burke-Jones.

John Merriman of Highworth, competing for Wales, winning the silver medal in the Empire Games six mile championship held at Cardiff Arms Park, 1958. Dave Power of Australia, the gold medallist, is on the inside.

Meet of the Vale of White Horse (Cricklade) Hunt, Market Place, *c.* 1910.

Highworth Youth Club Netball Team, Council School, *c.* 1952. Beryl Woodbridge is about to shoot.

Highworth Cricket Club, 1950. This occasion was a match against Moredon Royal Oak for the Morse Shield. Back row, left to right: P. McFall, N. (Dick) Bradford, P. Hind, M. Bond, A. Skull, S. Heydon, G. Tanner. Front row: J. Archer, D. Woodman, J. Cook (captain), R. Brock, L. Cox.

The original cricket pavilion's remains being surveyed by the groundsman John Ely, 1977. The pavilion was destroyed by fire during Halloween.

Highworth Cricket Club Presentation Dinner, 1958. Graham Tanner is being presented with the batting award by Mrs Evans, the wife of the Wiltshire County Cricket Captain.

Programme of Highworth Motorcycle and Light Car Club grass track races.

Enthusiasts' special train, Station Road, 1954.

Enthusiasts' brake van tour, Highworth station, May 1961. Note the Austin A55 Cambridge parked outside the station and the stationmaster's house (far right).

Goods shed, Highworth station. Built around 1897, this was the largest building on the line, although there is little evidence of its use.

Mixed train climbing the Butts Bank into Highworth station, early twentieth century.

Aerial view of the deserted
village at Eastrop. Eastrop Farm
is at the bottom right.

Major George Allen with his de Havilland 'Puss Moth' monoplane, *Maid of the Mist,*
c. 1937. This aircraft was used for the aerial photography of the Highworth 'circles' (crop
marks indicating evidence of medieval settlements) and the deserted village at Eastrop.

Berkshire Aviation Tours, East Hanney, late 1920s. The Berkshire Aviation Tours provided flying shows throughout the area, including Highworth.

A Mignet H.M. 'Pon du Ciel' (Flying Flea). This aircraft was built by E.H. Gray of Swindon and was flown from fields near The Freke Arms in 1936 and 1937.

Airship R101 on its flight over Highworth, 1 October 1930. On 7 October it had a fatal crash near Beauvais in France, on its projected flight to India, which resulted in the death of fifty-four passengers and crew.

Kenneth Annable, curator of Devizes Museum, c. 1960. An expert on the Roman period, he is examining a skeleton discovered during excavations for the building of Wrde Hill.

Barbara Humphries, Park Avenue, May 1958. At the age of nineteen, Barbara delivered her mother's fifth baby while awaiting the arrival of the ambulance.

'The Gang', 24 April 1921. Those present include Ralph Frankis. The photograph was taken by Jack Silk.

SECTION TWO

The Villages Around Highworth

Hannington station, soon after the nationalization of the rail system, late 1940s. The carriages are in GWR and British Rail livery.

The photograph above and those opposite show some of the events held at Hannington Hall in celebration of the Silver Jubilee of King George V and Queen Mary, 1935.

Cycling in the grounds of Hannington Hall, before the First World War.

Church Avenue, Hannington. This fine avenue of immemorial elms was decimated by Dutch elm disease in the late 1960s and early 1970s.

Interior of the church of St John the Baptist, Hannington.

Members of the Hussey-Freke family enjoying a picnic on the Hannington Hall estate, in the period prior to the First World War.

Members of the Hussey-Freke family embarking for a trip round the grounds of Hannington Hall in one of the estate's Wiltshire wagons, *c*. 1910.

The Vicarage, Hannington.

Domestic staff, Hannington Hall, *c.* 1900.

The Round House at the junction of the Thames & Severn Canal with the River Thames, Inglesham, *c.* 1900.

Victorian chromograph of the Round House, Inglesham, *c.* 1880.

Halfpenny Bridge over the River Thames, marking the county boundary between Wiltshire and Gloucestershire. The piles of the bridge were built on faggots and examination after the war showed no damage despite the heavy wartime traffic.

The toll-house, Halfpenny Bridge, from the Highworth side of the river. The cost of the toll is enshrined in the name of the bridge.

Porch of the Norman church of St John the Baptist, Inglesham. This church was beloved of William Morris of Kelmscott.

St Andrew's church, Sevenhampton, *c.* 1930.

Warneford Place, Sevenhampton, from the front lawn, *c.* 1930.

Warneford Place, Sevenhampton, from the lake, *c.* 1930. This was originally the home of the Warneford family, later that of Lord Banbury and more recently that of Ian Fleming, the author of the James Bond novels.

Commemorative print from the *Boys' Own Paper*. This shows Flight Sub-Lieutenant Reginald Warneford destroying the Zeppelin LZ37 over Ghent on 7 June 1915. For this feat he was awarded the Victoria Cross. The print sadly owes much to artistic licence.

Police controlling traffic, South Marston. This was necessary to allow passage of the fuselage of a Short Stirling to the flight sheds.

A Short Stirling being rolled out of Flight Shed 2, ready for its test flight, *c.* 1943.

Testing the undercarriage of a Short Stirling at Flight Shed 2, *c.* 1943.

Vickers Armstrong works, South Marston, *c.* 1950.

Supermarine Spitfire 24s under construction, South Marston, *c.* 1945.

Typical cottages of South Marston, 1930s. These are the Old Tannery Residence (top left), Cambria Cottage (top right), Rose Cottage (bottom left) and Dryden Cottage, the home of Alfred Williams, the 'Hammerman Poet' (bottom right).

Thatched cottage, Stanton Fitzwarren, *c.* 1940.

The old mill, Stanton Fitzwarren, *c*. 1920.

Distant view of the village of Stanton Fitzwarren.

St Leonard's church, Blunsdon.

Blunsdon station on the Midland and South Western Joint Railway, 1930s. This is now part of the Swindon and Cricklade Railway.

Meet of the Vale of White Horse (Cricklade) Hunt at the Coldharbour public house, March 1892.

Blunsdon St Andrew in the winter snows, 1946.

The 'forked elm', Highworth to Blunsdon road, c. 1950. This tree gave its name to the hill at this point. A wych elm, it eventually succumbed to Dutch elm disease and the bole was finally burned by vandals.

The Highworth 'Bunk', returning to Swindon, *c.* 1950. The train has stopped while the Cricklade Road level-crossing is opened.

Keeper's hut, Cricklade Road level-crossing, *c.* 1950. The crossing was generally unmanned.

SECTION THREE

Stratton St Margaret

Arkell's Kingsdown Brewery, 1930s.

James Arkell, founder of
Arkell's Kingsdown Brewery.

Arkell's Kingsdown Brewery delivery lorry, *c.* 1930.

The White Hart public house, Lower Stratton, *c*. 1920.

Later photograph, *c*. 1950, of Kingsdown crossroads and The Kingsdown public house.

Post Office, Stratton St Margaret, *c*. 1920. The Crown public house is on the far left.

Aerial view of Stratton Workhouse, *c*. 1935. Ermin Street is running from left to right, and the Quadrangle is being built on the far right. Note the open fields extending from Ermin Street.

The famous 'willow' tree, Ermin Street, *c.* 1935. In fact this was not a willow but a lime. It fulfilled the role of a meeting-place for the village, but sadness also surrounds the tree: a young Canadian pilot lost his life when his Spitfire crashed here.

Watercolour of the Wiltshire and Berkshire Canal, Lower Stratton.

Kingsdown crossroads, *c.* 1910.

Upper Stratton Senior School, as originally built in 1936. The modern design of the school led to rumours of its use as a hospital in the event of numerous air-raid casualties in a future war.

Stratton station and pagoda shelter, *c.* 1966.

Busy coal yard, Stratton station, 1966.

The staff of the Upper Stratton Secondary Modern School, *c.* 1948. Back row, left to right: Mrs E. Iles, -?-, R. Wellens, L. Owens, D. Iles, Mrs M. Saunders, Miss Eddolls, J. Gregory, G. Furkins, -?-, -?-. Second row: R. Cox, Miss H. Ward, S. Smith, Miss J. Perry, W. Flux (Deputy Headmaster), A.D. Padfield (Headmaster), Mrs G. Beasley, ? Brown, -?-, ? Barnes, -?-.

Girls of Upper Stratton Secondary Modern School, 1950. Their school dresses were made in their needlework lessons. Those present include Margery Hill, Mrs G. Beasley (senior mistress), Beryl Woodbridge, Beryl Styles, Carol Overington.

Pupils of Upper Stratton Secondary Modern School, *c.* 1949. Those present include Brian Smith, David Lovegrove, ? Tuck, John Barrett, Margery Hill.

Upper Stratton Secondary Modern School Under-fifteen Netball Team, 1955. Back row, left to right: M. Rolfe, S. Druett, Miss M. Townsend, R. Butcher, C. Shakespeare. Front row: -?- , G. Staines, -?-.

North Wiltshire Schools Area Athletics Championships, 1949. This is the final of the 220 yards. D. Rickets was the winner, with B. Smith in second place. Both came from Upper Stratton Secondary Modern School.

English Schools' Championships, 1963. Left to right: Brian Edwards (hammer), Sandra Thomas (discus), Malcolm Haskins (hammer). These three represented Wiltshire Schools.

Upper Stratton Secondary Modern School Under-fifteen Football Team, 1948. Back row, left to right: J. Barrett, R. Carter, R. Keene, H. Gorton, ? Sansum, B. Smith, -?-, T. Dean. Front row: -?-, P. Guy, D. Lewis, P. Fuller, P. Webb.

Upper Stratton Secondary Modern School, winners of the Wiltshire Schools' Shield, 1949. Back row, left to right: -?-, J. Jefferies, ? Lane, ? Sansum; K. Walker, P. Webb, B. Smith, J. Barrett, -?-. Front row: C. Jones, P. Guy, D. Lovegrove, ? Carter, C. Tremblin.

Upper Stratton Secondary Modern School, winners of the Marlborough Six-a-Side Football, 1955. Back row, left to right: G. Tanner, D. Vowles, D. McIver, G. Littlechild. Front row: R. Woodruff, D. Gray, G. Skinner.

Brenda Gill of Green Road with her medals from the International Pentathlon in Holland, 1963. The medals are Team Gold and Individual Silver. The Individual Gold was won by Mary Peters, later the Gold Medal winner in the 1972 Olympics.

Stefan Gawluk of Upper Stratton, throwing the hammer, 1967. Stefan was Britain's top ranked youth (under-seventeen) hammer thrower that year.

Alan Kemp receiving the Colin Smith Cup for outstanding athletics performance from physical education master Graham Tanner, c. 1962.

Circuit training, Kingsdown High School, 1966.

SECTION FOUR
Faringdon

Faringdon, 1950s.

Nineteenth-century print of All Saints' parish church.

FRD.44.   THE CHURCH. FARINGDON.

All Saints' parish church. The central tower, although massive, is low in proportion to the church as a whole. The reason for this is the destruction of a noble spire by parliamentary troops when they besieged Faringdon in 1646.

Porch and vestigial tower of All Saints'
parish church.

Interior of All Saints' parish church, looking towards the chancel.

The
Old Town Hall,
Faringdon.

Few places in Berkshire can trace their history from so remote a period as Faringdon. The first Charter is dated 1218. The Saxon Kings had a residence here, wherein Edward the Elder died in 925 and a Castle was built in the reign of Stephen by the Earl of Gloucester, but was destroyed a few years after. During the Civil War Cromwell attacked the town, but was successfully resisted by the garrison, under Sir M. Rawdon.

Market day, before the First World War. Markets were held every Tuesday with a great cattle market on the first Tuesday in every month, described by *Cassey's Directory* of 1869 as being 'well attended with cattle of every kind'.

Market day, *c.* 1910. As well as the Tuesday market, Cassey reported 'an annual horse fair on the 13th February, and statute fairs on the Tuesday before and Tuesday after Old Michaelmas Day'.

An extremely crowded Market Place, *c.* 1920. The reason for this display of motor-cars is not known.

Market Place, Faringdon, *c.* 1920, looking towards All Saints' parish church. The Crown Hotel, a Tudor coaching inn, is on the far left.

Market Place from the church, showing the Portwell (the water source in the centre of Market Place), *c.* 1910.

Seventeenth-century Market House, looking towards Market Place, *c.* 1960.

Market Hall, Faringdon, *c*. 1910.

Market Place, early 1960s.

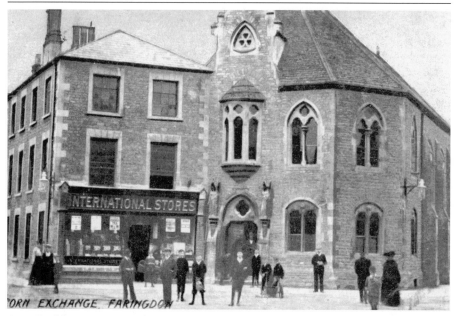

Corn Exchange, *c.* 1920. This was built in 1863 with a reading room attached, as well as space for a savings bank.

Gloucester Street, looking towards Lechlade Road, *c.* 1960. The Corn Exchange is on the immediate left, and the cinema behind The Volunteer public house is on the right.

Lechlade Road, 1920s.

Cottage Hospital, Faringdon, *c.* 1920. With vastly improved transport, the need for a hospital in the town has passed, so it now serves as the local health centre.

London Street, Faringdon, looking down the hill towards the town centre, *c.* 1920.

Coxwell Street, Faringdon, *c.* 1920.

London Street from Market Place, mid-1920s. The Bell Hotel is on the immediate right.

'Sit-down' protest against traffic through the centre of Faringdon and in favour of the A420 bypassing the town, 1960s.

Nineteenth-century print of Faringdon Lodge.

An equine guest at tea with Lord Berners, Faringdon House, 1930s.

The BRICK KILNS,
FARINGDON, BERKS

MR. GEORGE JOHN DYKE

Has received instructions from Mrs. H. GODFREY (who is leaving), to Sell by Auction, on the premises, as above, on

WEDNESDAY, SEPTEMBER 25, 1901

At 1 for 2 o'clock, the whole of the Stock of

Building Bricks, Drain Pipes, Trade Utensils, &c.

ALSO THE

Live & Dead FARMING STOCK

As follows :—

43,000 BUILDING BRICKS, 82,000 UNBURNED DITTO,

7,300 Drain Pipes, 2,000 Roofing & other Tiles,

900 FLOWER POTS, quantity of Coping Bricks, Ridge Crests, Gutter Tiles, Lime Stone, &c., 3 PIPE-MAKING MACHINES, & other Utensils,

The Agricultural Implements

Including 3 Wagons, 7 Carts, Cambridge Roll, Sets of Harrows, Horse Hoe, Iron Skim, Horse Rake, Haymaking Machine, Mowing Machine, Harness, &c.

2 WORKING CART HORSES AND 2 COLTS,

30 Head of POULTRY, RICK of MEADOW HAY (to go off), &c., described as follows :—

CATALOGUE.

Pipes, Bricks, Tiles, &c.

Plant and Utensils.

Farming Stock.

Implements, &c.

Cart Horses.

Poultry.

Hay (to go off)

Catalogues may be obtained at the place of Sale, and of the Auctioneer, Faringdon, Berks.

C. Luker & Co., Printers, Faringdon

Bill of sale for the Faringdon brick kilns, 1901.

Single coach train at Faringdon, Christmas Eve, 1951.

Railway enthusiasts' excursion, headed by a 1910 Churchward-built locomotive, Faringdon station, 26 April 1959.

Coal wagon owned by W.S. Clarke and employed on the Uffington–Faringdon branch line, prior to the Second World War.

Station staff, Faringdon, c. 1910. Back row, left to right: E. Bonner, ? McKenzie, B. Vaughan, -?-, F. Dibden, -?-, J. Berryman, E. Glanville, A. Taylor, J. Hammond, -?-. Front row: S. Norton, H.W. Tidsbury, L. Crook (stationmaster).

Meet of the Old Berkshire Hunt, Faringdon House, 1930s.

Meet of the Old Berkshire Hunt, Charney Bassett, 1940s.

Meet of the Old Berkshire Hunt, Buckland House, mid-1930s.

Old Berkshire Hunt Point-to-Point, Faringdon, mid-1930s.

Nineteenth-century print of Faringdon Folly. From here Cassey said, 'on a clear day, thirty parish churches may be seen, and [it is] a favourite promenade, commanding beautiful and extensive views of the surrounding country'.

Advertising poster of the 1930s showing Faringdon Folly from the River Thames. By this time Lord Berners had built the tower, which lays claim to being the last true folly in the country.

SECTION FIVE
The Vale Villages

Interior of the tithe barn, Great Coxwell. The influence of ecclesiastical architecture is clear. Note the Berkshire wagons complete with ladders (on the wagon in the foreground one of the ladders has been replaced with a hurdle).

The tithe barn, Great Coxwell. This barn was built by the monks of Beaulieu, to whom King John had given the manor. It dates from the first half of the thirteenth century, and is 150 feet long, nearly 50 feet wide and more than 50 feet high.

The tithe barn, Great Coxwell. The barn uses an elaborate and sophisticated system of roof construction and is clearly the work of highly skilled carpenters.

Coleshill House, shown here in the 1930s, was the training headquarters of the Auxiliary Units from mid-1940. The Auxiliary Units were intended to remain behind in the coastal areas in the event of an invasion by Germany and to carry out guerrilla warfare.

Officers serving with the Auxiliary Units, Coleshill House, January 1942.

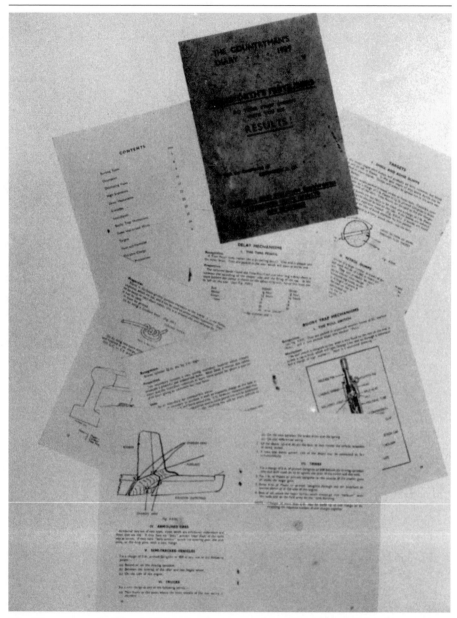

The 'Countryman's Diary'. This was the instructional booklet used by the Auxiliary Units while under training at Coleshill House.

The main gates, Coleshill House,
Highworth–Faringdon road.

The main staircase, Coleshill House.

Part of the village green and the village stores, Coleshill, *c.* 1960.

Estate cottages, Coleshill, *c.* 1960. Coleshill remains an estate village with no additional building, and is effectively a 'planned village'.

Clock House, Coleshill estate, 1960.

Strattenborough Castle Farm, Coleshill. This is in effect a folly, the castellations disguising the farm buildings. From Coleshill House it can just be made out on the horizon.

Coleshill Athletic Football Club, Winners of Division Two Swindon and District League, 1950/1 Back row, left to right: L. Brown, -?-, C. Brown. Middle row: A. Pedley, -?-, P. Whitman, F. Brown, G. Wright, G. Cox, F. Caswell. Front row: P. Page, J. Smith, A. Skull, D. Caswell, A. Woodbridge.

Lockheed Hercules from RAF Lyneham, carrying out heavy-load dropping at RAF Watchfield, c. 1970.

The Green, Watchfield, *c.* 1920. This village was originally a township in the parish of Shrivenham.

High Street, Watchfield, *c.* 1920.

Hill Road, Watchfield, mid-1920s.

Shrivenham station, 1840s. In 1846 the followers of the Broome v. Terry fight, brought to Shrivenham from London by the GWR, decamped and caused a disturbance of the peace. This resulted in arrests by the local constabulary.

High Street, Shrivenham, *c.* 1920.

Park Cottages, Shrivenham, at the entrance to Beckett Park, *c.* 1920. The park is presently the Royal Military College of Science, but was previously the Shrivenham American University and early 63 Officer Cadet Training Unit (OCTU) Royal Artillery.

High Street, Shrivenham, 1960s.

The centre of Buscot village, *c.* 1965.

Buscot House from the north-west.

Interior of St John's parish church, Buscot.

Acknowledgements

I extend my most grateful thanks to my wife, Maureen, for her continued patience and forebearance in my search for photographs and ephemera of Highworth and district, and in the preparation of this compilation; also to Brian Earl for all his help and assistance in the reproduction of photographs and to Mrs Andree Amos for her secretarial skills.

I am also indebted to Mrs Beryl Woodbridge-Harmon and Mr Jim Wilmot, Mr John Ely, Mr Brian Smith, Mr Fred Hill, Mr Geoffrey Crowe, the late Mr Peter Stanley for the loan of photographs for copying, and to the many people of Highworth and the surrounding area who by their interest and enthusiasm have contributed to the production of this second book of photographs of the area.

Finally my thanks must also go to Mr Derek White, Mr Fred Stevens, Mr Pete Sheldon and Mrs Moxon for continuing to produce postcards and ephemera of the district for me to add to my collection.

St Michael's parish church, the churchyard and the church alley (right).